TO _____

FROM _____

_____

_____

I L♥VE MY GRANDPA!

A *For Better or For Worse*® Book

by Lynn Johnston

Poem by Andie Parton

**Andrews McMeel
Publishing**
Kansas City

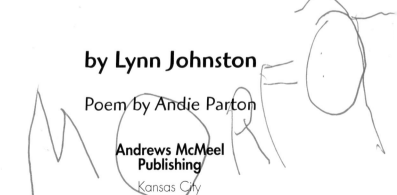

♥

We have a special something,
My grandfather and I.

He says that I'm his apple,
The one that's in his eye!

♥

I love to visit Grandpa.
He doesn't mind the noise.
He rocks me in his big old chair,
And I think he likes my toys!

♥

I look a lot like Grandpa,
At least, that's what they said.
I've got his ears and eyes and chin,
I even have his head!

If I should fill my diaper

The days I'm babysat . . .

He lets my grandma change me,
My grandpa's nice like that.

My grandpa says I'm grumpy,

It's just a little flap . . .

But Grandma says he's worse than me
And now we *both* need naps!

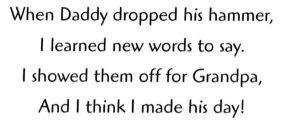

When Daddy dropped his hammer,
I learned new words to say.
I showed them off for Grandpa,
And I think I made his day!

♥

I know the tales he tells me
Are absolutely true,
'Cause when my grandma rolls her eyes
I see she's dazzled, too!

♥

Grandpa is no techie,

It's mostly geek to him . . .

So when we play computer games

I have to let him win.

I drive my grandpa's tractor.
He sits me on his lap.
We never really start it up,
But don't tell Grandma that!

Lots of things don't bother Gramps,

Bad hair or mismatched shoes . . .

And he would never wash my face
Like Mom and Grandma do!

♥

A quickie wipe around my face,
A pat-dry with his shirt,
I look just fine to Grandpa
'Cause he doesn't notice dirt.

♥

Sometimes he picks my clothes for me,
Not always a good fit.
He mixes up my stripes and plaids,
I'm quite the fashion hit!

♥

We have a lot in common,
My grandfather and I.
We both love grilled cheese sandwiches
And watching life go by.

Whenever we go walking,

He's never in a rush . . .

We follow bugs and look at clouds,

All Grandpa's favorite stuff.

When trials and tribulations
Become too much for me,
I find that Grandpa's shoulder is
The perfect place to be.

My gramps believes in magic
And dreams that can come true.
He said, "I wished upon a star
Then I was blessed with you!"

I love my grandpa!

For Better or For Worse® is distributed by Universal Press Syndicate.

I Love My Grandpa! copyright © 2006 by Lynn Johnston Productions, Inc. All rights reserved. Printed in Singapore. No part of this book may be used or reproduced in any manner whatsoever without written permission except in the case of reprints in the context of reviews. For information, write Andrews McMeel Publishing, an Andrews McMeel Universal company, 4520 Main Street, Kansas City, Missouri 64111.

06 07 08 09 10 TWP 10 9 8 7 6 5 4 3 2 1

ISBN-13: 978-0-7407-5679-5
ISBN-10: 0-7407-5679-6

www.FBorFW.com
www.andrewsmcmeel.com

Attention: Schools and Businesses

Andrews McMeel books are available at quantity discounts with bulk purchase for educational, business, or sales promotional use. For information, please write to: Special Sales Department, Andrews McMeel Publishing, 4520 Main Street, Kansas City, Missouri 64111.